# STAY FRESH
# STAY BLESSED
## SUCCESS TRACKING!!

*A Journal to Unlock Your Best & Stop Slacking!*

A simple guide to get you from where you are
to where you want to be and beyond!

## DOUGIE FORLANO

Co-author

_____

Your name
Phone #_____

# STAY FRESH
## STAY BLESSED
### SUCCESS TRACKING!!

*A Journal to Unlock Your Best & Stop Slacking!*

A simple guide to get you from where you are
to where you want to be and beyond!

Dougie Forlano inspires and energizes anyone and everyone when simply entering the room. Every day, Dougie lives to his fullest, drinking every last drop of nectar of wisdom, joy, generosity and gratitude that life provides. Dougie has just pulled back the curtain and opened the vault, showing you exactly how he lives so fully. He pours out his love, energy, passion, hope and belief that people can become their greatest selves for anyone who will receive it. Dougie's newest fast track personal action guide, Stay Fresh Stay Blessed, is The BLUEPRINT of how he has achieved so much in such a short time. The first time we met he had 4 leather bound journals with every single page filled. I knew they were valuable then, and now I realize how precious and activating they were for Dougie, and Stay Fresh Stay Blessed invites, challenges and enables you to experience the Fountain of Youth that feeds Dougie every day!

*- Steven Rowell*
*President, Accelerated Ventures*
*Author of Success from the Inside Out; Jumpstart Your Creativity and The Five Minute Secret*

"Doug Forlano is one of the most passionate and giving people I have ever met. His enthusiasm for other people's success is contagious! This book is a tool to tap into your own passion, utilizing the tools of a master inspirer."

*Chris Hawker - Inventor, Founder & CEO for Trident Designs/Cofounder Next Level Trainings*

Dougie exudes inspiration wherever he goes. Anytime I have a chance to interact with him and hear his perspective, I'm upgraded at least two levels of purpose driven passion. His message is contagious in the best way possible!

*- JP Sears, Comedian,*
*Speaker & Author of How to be Ultra Spiritual*

Dougie is a young man that fully represents our core message of LEARN IT - LIVE IT- GIVE IT! He is learning what it takes to live the life of his dreams, he is LIVING IT fully each day and through his work and books like this one sharing the best of what he knows with you! Good work Dougie!

*- Jairek Robbins,*
*Performance Coach*

"Dougie is a fire ball of constant energy, committed learner & a 5 star human. I've been around some of the most successful influencers on the planet and Dougie is headed there with this tool!

He is a sponge and this Success Tracker is a reflection of him and how he is able to do it. Now you can tap into that power too!"

*- Larry Benet,*
*Cheif connector & cofounder of SANG*

"Journaling has been one of the most powerful self-development tools I've used. It's been apart of my daily ritual for years as a means of helping to actualize my potential and strive towards life mastery. This tool from Dougie will support you in Mastery as well!"

*- Stefan Pylarinos author,*
*speaker blogger and creator of Project Life Mastery*

"I journal every morning in a certain way. The morning time is for you! Journaling is super important to set intention, super important to claim a great space and super important before you pick up your freaking phone! You put you 1st with Journaling! 5..4..3..2..1 Go!"

*- Mel Robbins*
*Speaker and author of the 5 Second Rule*

"I've had the privilege of coaching Doug over the last year in an extraordinary Mastery of Leadership training program. His artistry and creativity with words are actually surpassed by his passion and love for people. As an up and comer in the work of transformation, I have no doubt Doug will make indelible mark."

*- Michael Strasner*
*Trainer/Coach/Author*
*#1 Amazon Best Seller of Living in the Skinny Branches*

"Dougie delivers again! Another amazing Opportunity to accelerate your life forward and upward by maximizing the moments in your life.

This Success Tracker is a straight pathway to the top if you take on the challenge to use what's inside it will bring all that's inside you alive and your best self will rise up with greater results than you can imagine. Don't miss out and not practice what's within this powerful workbook."

*- James Swanwick,*
*CEO of Swanwick Sleep and 30 Day No Alcohol*
*Challenge.*

"You got to journal! You got to write. Observation means you are paying attention in life. Through writing things down you will grow. Keep following the man Dougie with this right here"

*- Author,*
*speaker and celebrity coach Tim Storey*

"I think journaling is one of the best practices and habits you can develop. I do it almost daily. This tool will assist you in following through. Dougie is an inspiration and a blessing."

*- Dr.Joe Martin Speaker,*
*Author & Certified Man Builder at RealMenConnect.com*

Dougie is a Dynamic leader who thrives off of connecting others and seeing others reach success. This journal is a absolute game changer and I highly recommend anyone who wants to get to the next level to get one.

*- Nehemiah Davis*
*Founder of Circle Of Greatness Academy*

"I have witnessed extreme growth, and loving community contributions from Doug. He is an energetic, caring leader up to BIG things in the World. A true gift & Inspiration just like this new book that I'm committed to using to level up my life"

*- Vinny Vegan*
*Founder of Gangster Vegan Organics*

"The practices in the Stay Fresh Stay Blessed Success Tracker will have you crush it consistently and dominate each day! This tool is a secret weapon that goes beyond the grind. Dougie is one of a kind and this book is too and designed in a one of a kind way that we all can learn from. If we act on it!"

*Brandon Carter founder of Bro Labs*

"From the moment I met Dougie Forlano I knew he was a force of nature. I have never met a more generous man! Everyone that encounters this loving, electrifying and passionate soul is blessed to have met him. The world now gets to learn from Dougie Forlano through his extraordinary Stay Fresh Stay Blessed Success Tracking System. Get ready to turn your dreams into reality!"

*- Chris Lee*
*Trainer/Author*
*Transform your life 10 Principles of*
*Abundance and Prosperity*

# ROHN: WHY YOU SHOULD KEEP A JOURNAL

Be a student of your own life, your own future, your own destiny.

Jim Rohn the #1 business Philosopher.

"If you're serious about becoming a wealthy, powerful, sophisticated, healthy, influential, cultured and unique individual, keep a journal—don't trust your memory. When you listen to something valuable, write it down. When you come across something important, write it down.

I used to take notes on pieces of paper, torn-off corners and backs of old envelopes. I wrote ideas on restaurant placemats, long sheets, narrow sheets, little sheets and pieces of paper thrown in a drawer. And the best way to organize all those ideas was to keep a journal.

So I became a buyer of blank books. People found it interesting that I would buy a blank book. "Twenty-six dollars for a blank book, why would you pay that?" they'd say. Well, the reason I paid it was to challenge myself to find something worth $26 to put in there. But if you ever got a hold of one of my journals, you wouldn't have to look very far to discover that it's worth more than this.

Keeping a journal is so important. In fact, it is one of three important treasures to leave behind for the next generation"

Now I too quickly learned writing in the journal was far more powerful, efficient and I no longer had a pile of napkins, placemats and post-its to worry about. You will also discover writing consistently, whether daily or weekly, is critical to experiencing the power of journaling.

I learned after collecting tons of insights the best way to keep all those ideas and any notes in one place is to utilize a journal- far better than using your notes in a cell phone. There is something about the pen to paper that is organic and perhaps even magical! Also consider the risk of losing all your data if your cellphone or tablet crashes and your app wasn't automatically storing to a cloud server. Finally, on your down days, whereever you are, thumbing through your past journal entries may ignite your spirit to get you back to your best self and on the positive track more quickly. Here are the 3 Treasures Jim Rohn my first online mentor spoke of and why Journaling is the most powerful of all!

# 1. YOUR PICTURES.

"Don't be lazy in capturing an event. How long does it take to snap a photo? A fraction of a second. How long does it take to miss an event? A fraction of a second. So don't miss out on the moments—when you're gone, they'll keep the memories alive."

On this note as you keep this journal I invite you to plug in and paste a picture or 2 of yourself! One for when you start your journal, and another for towards the end! **Also you can use Instagram or Facebook to document you journaling Journaling journey as well!!** Every blue moon or so I go back and see how far I've come! Pictures are powerful and will aid in your life's masterpiece you are creating so don't be camera shy! Trust me, you are the ONLY person worrying so much about how you look in pictures. Everyone else sees you and your spirit. Don't believe me? Remember the last time you saw pictures of friends: did you sit there critically analyzing their hair, skin, weight and eye color? Or were you more struck by the spirit of the image or what was happening in the image. Exactly! It is the same for everyone else viewing you--forget about the trolls and the haters! If you really want to make a powerful, inspiring, lasting mark, videos and vlogs are awesome as well!!

## 2. YOUR LIBRARY.

Jim Rohn also says, "This is the library which taught you, instructed you, helped you defend your ideals. It helped you develop a philosophy. It helped you become wealthy, powerful, healthy, sophisticated and unique.

**Your library—the books that instructed you and fed your mind and your soul—is one of the greatest gifts you can leave behind."**
--Dougie Forlano

## 3. YOUR JOURNALS.

Journals are the priceless vault of ideas you picked up and the information you meticulously gathered through the course of your journey. Of the three, journal writing is one of the *greatest* indications you're a serious student. Taking pictures—that's pretty easy. Buying a book at a bookstore—that's pretty easy. It is a little more challenging to be a student of your own life, your own future, your own destiny."

Take the time to write notes and to keep a journal. You'll be so glad you did. What a treasure to leave behind when you go. What a treasure to enjoy today!

I started journaling daily on December 1st, 2012. I did it for 4 years straight without missing a day! I have the proof. What it did for me was create much more than just some success. It also allowed me to be rigorous, focused, disciplined, structured and organized. Daily journaling created joy, confidence, and passion that made my relationships magnificent. I still follow this strategy and system today currently after updating it to its most effective version which you now have in your hands!

**"This is a real commitment; this is happening through hell or high water," I said to myself. "Even if I get my arms chopped off I will use my mouth to write what happened each day and hold myself high."**
--Dougie Forlano

Since delivering on this declaration of daily action toward a habit, it became automatic and my spirit was ecstatic. My spirit was soaring because I was proud, grateful for being in integrity with my word. Therefore, my self-worth way up, and the same will happen for you, as well as increasing benefits for you because there are tons. Here are several:

- Captured memories to reflect back on, to get inspired from as you see what exactly happened and how you felt
- Stress relief
- Addition of clarity
- Showing yourself and the world that you are serious
- Creation of an awareness in your life, an ability to see what you truly want and what holds you back
- A gift to the world and your family when you pass away

# TABLE OF CONTENTS

# WHAT IS *STAY FRESH STAY BLESSED?*

*"We are fresh, ripe and new to each moment-
-we are able to let go of the past, which may
not serve us and step into the HERE and
NOW and move forward from there."*
--Dougie Forlano

This phrase is simple. It means every moment is sacred. One day during my internship at the world famous Strength Camp, the owner and founder and truly a mentor to many men all over the planet came in and asked everybody at the gym if they wanted to go to a country concert to see Florida Georgia Line. Now at this time I didn't really care for Country music at all! I'd personally much rather see and listens to some Hip Hop or Rock and Roll!

Surprisingly everybody else felt the same or already had plans and passed on the free tickets and tailgating this Friday summer night but not me! No way would I miss out on an opportunity to hang out with my hero, so I joyfully said, "I'm in," and we headed out. We had a blast, and it was a memory I'll never forget.

A couple weeks later we did it again! This time, we stopped by his home, and I was reading a book from his library. In his favorite book "The Essential Writing of Ralph Waldo Emerson", a specific phrase stood out to me--it was highlighted in bright yellow. It mentioned something along the lines of how every moment is sacred when we choose to see the power in it. Sitting at the tailgate later, I shared this with Elliott, and he said, "Well, yes! Last time we were here it was a sacred experience; the people over there are having a sacred experience (pointing to the people nearby)."

Elliot continued, "You know what this moment right now is? A holy moment, and in a couple moments we will be having another sacred experience. Do you know why?" I shrugged my Shoulders, and he said, "Because it's new, it's never happened before." I interpreted this as such a gift and blessing. A light bulb went off in my mind because the truth of his words can be experienced when we are present, grateful and aware to the Fresh moments happening all the time.

Only when we see the blessing in it, we come back to our truth-- we are fresh, ripe and new to each moment; we are able to let go of the past which may not serve us and step into the HERE and NOW and move forward from there. What a blessing this is! This is why I say, "Stay Fresh Stay Blessed," and this book of yours will help you rediscover and amplify, and, hopefully, then embrace, one again, your authentic awesome YOU!

To summarize, it's simple: "Stay fresh, stay blessed" is not just a saying; it is a numerological anchor to pull you into the facts... you are already a blessing; there's tons to be grateful for in the new; and this never happened before. The moment is now. Honor it with greater self awareness and presence: "You live a life worth living." In short, it means to be grateful and present...YOUR LIFE IS NOW!

# VISION/WHY AND PURPOSE ARE THE STARTING POINT

**"Our future is dictated by what we do today."**
--Dougie Forlano

Why exist if you don't have a purpose? Let's get clear on yours right here, right now.

I had the epiphany sitting in college: it's not what we get that matters, but who we become in the progress towards our future. I realized that our future is dictated by what we do today, the joy in life came from the growth from taking action on massive goals based on what I wanted. Those challenges stretched and sharpened me into a greater version of me.

If one does not have a plan, often he or she gets carried away by life. Crisis after crisis happens like waves in the ocean. We get smacked around, which limits and hurts us. Although we learn lessons, we learn them the hard way, and we are not maximizing our time.

But with this book you're creating, you're in control as the surfer! You can rise above like a dolphin or a shark only if you put your heart into this.

Your ceilings will become your floor when you're committed to be senior to your circumstances. Ultimately, it is about being proactive on offense, designing the life of your dreams and having an absolute blast in the process!!

I want you to avoid asking the question "How did I even get here?" a year or 2 from now, and instead, start creating the life you want each day. YES that means today is a part of this.

**"If you don't have a plan, you fall into someone else's plan. And guess what they got planned for you: Not much."**
--Jim Rohn

Rohn also says, "If you don't run the day, the day runs you."

Without a plan you just get whatever shows up, and again, this journal is for those who want to create what they want. How awesome! You get to manifest who you are, what you do, and want you will have!

I bet you'd agree when someone passes away and we are at their funeral, gathered around to celebrate and honor that person, people don't care what possessions he owned or money they had. More so, the value is placed on who we were and the qualities in our character, what we were about, the life we led and the difference we made!

If I am not an empowering enough example, this tool I've been using for the last 5 years works, KNOW that most high performing leaders living an incredibly great life whom we look up to use some form of Journaling as well! Let's take Oprah for example. She has used what she calls her diary. She got super specific on what she wanted, she wrote it down, and if you asked Oprah her vision, she could tell you. The same is true for any influencer or leader that plays at a high level!

They have used some type of notebook or recording device to monitor their vision to see if they are on track and better believe they had that vision of theirs front and center. I believe you must too if you want to see it come to fruition.

Here is the key about all of this. When it is written, it becomes real! Benjamin Franklin knew what he wanted and where he was going, and let's keep it "100" like the bill he is on...it works! (Keeping it 100 means the absolute truth)

Therefore, know the importance of writing down your vision. Ben Franklin also kept a journal! You know who else did? Leonardo Da Vinci, Sir Richard Branson, Tony Robbins and the list goes on and on. They were also all precise about their purpose. Get clear on your top purpose for keeping this Success Tracker with you at all times, and what your vision for your life is.

What do you want? What will make you happy? What life do you want to lead? Write your dream down that you'd love to live to see come true while you are on the planet. Keep focused on a purpose that pulls you out of bed and pushes you forward.

It is actually very easy to discover! What I have for you is an effective tool called "The Life Purpose Exercise" from Jack Canfield's book *"The Success Principles."*

This is a short simple exercise you can do right now. So write now...

1. What are 3 gifts, skills or great qualities about you?

_____

2. How do you like expressing them? What are 2 or 3 ways

_____

3. And what kind of world and environment would you like to be in?

Assume the world is perfect right now. What does this world look like? How is everyone interacting with everyone else? What does it feel like? Write your answer as a statement, in the present tense, describing the ultimate condition, the perfect world as you see it and feel it. Remember a perfect world is a fun place to be.

Steven Rowell, one of my mentors and dear friends, asks it this way:

**"If you could wake up every morning, get
dressed and walk into the next room, who
would you want to see there; what you
be doing together; and what passion and
purpose would you be living? What difference
would you then be making?"**

Now put them all together and presto! Then share it with
passion to 5 people today!

Here is an example of my Vision/Purpose Statement:

**"My major purpose is to use my presence,
passion, care and intelligence to inspire,
connect, grow and give to others in a free,
fun, dynamic, compassionate, united and
loving way!"**
--Dougie Forlano

As you can tell I like to put a little extra sauce and spice
on mine! But you can create and adapt your purpose any-
way you want.

Later we will go into the nitty gritty and delight in the
details. However, that process creates the BIG picture
and can be powerful for some people. Another individual's WHY may be more direct such as, buy my mom a

new home, live by the beach debt free, be a great father, graduate from school with a 3.5 GPA or above. Whatever stage in life you are in, it's key to have that clear motive to drive you during difficult times and great times when you want to rest. Keeping your mission front and center is the foundation of living a Fresh and blessed life.

Now imagine how my beliefs, thoughts, choices, actions and results will change when I become crystal clear on how to live my purpose!

Take each piece of your Purpose Statement and write down all of the actions that demonstrate this piece of your Purpose Statement. For example, using my example, what specifically, will I do consistently to live these words?

*Presence:*
*Passion:*
*Care:*
*Intelligence:*
*Inspire:*
*Connect:*
*Grow:*
*Give:*

How do I consistently express all of this in the following way?

*Free:*
*Fun:*
*Dynamic:*
*Compassionate:*
*United:*
*Loving:*

# WHY IS THIS SO IMPORTANT TO ME?

Your Vision and Purpose focus on what you see in your future and the meaning and value you place in and from your own journey.

Answering the "Why?" question enables you to reach deeper into the reasons, drivers and catalysts of what you are doing to consistently live your Vision and Purpose.

Why do you want to live debt free? What will living debt free do for you? How will your own life experience be changed when you become debt free? How will you show up in the world? How will you impact the world around you? Why should anyone care? What "impossible" is now possible after living debt free?

Give yourself the gift of private time to ask yourself these questions for each item that comes up for you, similar to "live debt free."

Why do you wish to fulfill your purpose and vision this way?

———80CR———

**"People don't buy WHAT you do, they buy WHY you do it. And what you do simply proves what you believe."**
--Simon Sinek

———80CR———

# PERSONAL REFLECTION AND DISCOVERY GIFT

**Vision: An imagined idea or goal toward which one aspires.**

**What I see in my future, what is possible or worthy of pursuit and investment of time, energy and resources. What impact, change or enabling force is possible?**

**My Vision: Imagine...**

_____

_____

_____

Purpose: Why I am here. The meaning or value that comes from what I do. The expression, existence and being of my highest self in service to my highest values and human needs.

**My Purpose:**

Why: Why is the reason, cause or belief that inspires you to do what you do.

**My Why:**

To help you discover your Why, the reason that inspires you to do what you do, answer these questions for yourself: (from Matt Tod)

What energizes, inspires or moves me deeply or moves me to action?

Hey
When am I most happy?

_____

_____

If money didn't matter, how would I spend my time?
(Stephen Covey)

What's important to me?

_____

_____

Inspiration from start-up companies' "Why Statements":

**Why Build Asana?** Because it sucks to waste unnecessary time trying to communicate instead of getting work done. Asana

**Why Build Uber?** Because it sucks to be stranded without easy access to reliable transportation

**Why Build GoldieBlox?** Because girls are discouraged from building things, and we need to change that.

# DECLARATION OF INTERDEPENDENCE

Living in Philadelphia there is the sacred document of our country: "The Declaration of Independence" just down the street.

Make a vow now that this vision won't be achieved alone! In fact, nothing great ever was. Interdependence is a step above independence. Instead of 1+1=2 with a team of others who have your back, you hack life and turn 1+1 into 11! This is creating the abundant mindset that everyone can win and allowing others to be the wind beneath your wings as you fly high towards your best life and best self.

Now, think about your strengths and who else has similar gifts to yours. Can you all get together and brainstorm ways you can contribute to each individual's life purpose? What about a few weaknesses or things you're not as skilled with? Can you get support around that? This will rapidly accelerate your results and make life go much smoother. Stop banging your head against the wall trying to do it yourself in your own way and believing you're right about...those are manifestations of the ego which hold us back from our greatness. I only know because I've been banging my head against the wall so much I've cultivated a unicorn horn full of wisdom.

Why is it important for you to get support from others?

_____

_____

_____

_____

Now write your own declaration of Interdependence:

_____

_____

_____

_____

————ꝏCꙄ————

**"You are the average of the 5 people you spend the most time with."**
--Jim Rohn

————ꝏCꙄ————

We begin to behave and think like them in a very real way.

Now list the 5 people with whom you are currently most connected.

1. _____

2. _____

3. _____

4. _____

5. _____

And if you don't have 5, that's feedback for you to enable you to expand and create your vision.

Who are some people who have helped get you here and who will those next mentors be?

1. _____

2. _____

3. _____

4. _____

5. _____

6. _____

7. _____

8. _____

9. _____

10. _____

What are the reasons, excuses and stories I tell myself, keeping me from living a more interdependent life?

What are my limiting beliefs about trusting others or depending on others or letting go of control?

# MY DECLARATION OF INTERDEPENDENCE:

One example:

I will always seek to live and engage with others with humility, transparency, and vulnerability to create the most safe and trusting environment (space) possible for the other person(s). I honor that people don't argue with their own data, and it is my responsibility to ask more questions and listen rather than talk and tell. All great accomplishments are achieved through interdependence, and I will strive to be where my feet are, to actively listen, and to always serve and support the other person with good faith, whether he or she, in turn, helps me or not.

# MY DECLARATION OF
# INTERDEPENDENCE:

_____

_____

_____

_____

_____

_____

_____

_____

_____

_____

_____

_____

_____

_____

# VIRTUES LIST

---⊱⊰---

**This is YOUR L1fe!**
--Dougie Forlano

---⊱⊰---

I like to put the number 1 in replace of the "I" because it reminds me that I am here living as Dougie Forlano once! You got one shot at this. Let's make it count.

There is nothing more important than this right here. Discovering, adjusting, deciding and declaring your values based on your Vision. By consciously picking the values you will live by, you then can take better control of your life.

You will also become your best and be fulfilled from it. This is the force that pulls us in life. You will feel on purpose, think on purpose and move on purpose! This is a the tool to life by design not by default.

We go mostly by society's values, our family's or usually our own life experiences. They are placed upon us by life, rather than happening because we use our own power and consciously selecting them based on what we want to create, which we CAN DO and WILL DO in a few moments.

What does not work is being at the effect of life, unaware of our values. By life happening to us, it's like being picked up by the hurricane of our situations. We rarely are the cause. Well, when we choose our own values, we are enabled to enter the eye of the crazy chaos surrounding others' outside standards, and, instead, we are calm at the cause and are able to create new possibilities. This then allows us to dictate and operate by choice, not by chance and we then the bosses in charge of our own lives, own our lives! No one else owns us when we live in accordance with the truth that what we say matters most.

**"If you stand for nothing you'll
fall for anything"**
--Malcolm X

Tony Robbins said, in in my favorite book, *Awaken The Giant Within* "People don't have problems; they have values problems."

We already have what we value in some way no matter how small, and the best way to discover your values is to look at your results along with your actions AKA what you do most frequently. This all comes from our own thoughts; yet it goes deeper. Our character is created by our values. So this goes straight to the core!

Knowing our worth and value will allow us you to take the time to make a list of our top virtues to live by. Only those who care enough about themselves know they matter so much where they are razor sharp on what's non-negotiable. When we do that, we're bulletproof and can always bounce back because our characters will be so resilient and strong.

This reminds me of a quote I see daily where I live in South Philly on a powerful mural on a building that states **"Life tried to bury us, but we are the root and the seed."**

You see! This is your root system! This is your seed that will show you the result that you'll get! This is hacking the system. OF COURSE it's up to us to water them with work, fertilizing them with friendships that are supportive, sunshine that is our spiritual practices. Yet before that we get to till the soil! That consists of noticing what does not work and what you don't want. Then we will unlock what we want and can enjoy are harvest season to season and be even bigger givers. So what do you want—oranges, apples, eggplant? How about avocado, so you can creat guacamole?!

We need to know when individuals have different values. They think differently and, therefore, take different actions, which lead to different results.

It's never a matter of one's values being better than another's—since it depends on what a person wants to create, on the person's current environment and goals.

Your values change as your life situation changes. If you are out of school all of a sudden after graduating, they may shift or if you become a parent there is more responsibility and the order or even particular values may move around.

————————&OR————————

**Ultimately, understand what is best for you right now based on where you want to go.**
--Dougie Forlano

————————&OR————————

So what we now get to do first is assess our current values to see if they're supporting us what what we want to create.

Again adapting what you care about by finding some of your truth pulls you towards what you want rather than having to push so hard all the time. Get off the pain train and live with more flow instead of going with the flow randomly with how you feel and your environment. You know who goes with the flow? DEAD FISH. Let's not live by what was placed upon us, certainly use it but it's infinitely more powerful when we are at the cause of where we want to go and choosing what to focus our attention on. Before creating our values, first ask what's been most important to us? For us in our lives?

Whatever the first answer is write it down! The initial response is usually spot on! You don't need to over-analyze this, go with your *gut*, then see what else comes up next. Then ask again and again what else has been most important for me in my life?

Then each of us should notice the emotion we were after, understanding that there are means values and ends values.

What we do to get to what we want. Mostly we operate for a main core value that's at the top of our hierarchy. This typically filters all else.

For example, I choose growth; therefore, I took risks, traveled, invested in myself and took adventures. Comfort was not important, so I slept on couches and did not care as much about being cozy. However, health is also held high at the top, so it was rarely sacrificed.

Get clear that the order matters because you want to avoid taking 2 steps forward and 5 steps back. Prioritize what is most important to you. Therefore, when someone says he or she doesn't have time to study, workout, plan whatever it is, it is because he or she doesn't value the action behind that: health, learning, strategizing, or whatever value is associated.

Now it's time to take action on this process. It does not have to be perfect. A person who has values and knows them is better off than one who does not. Look back at your vision you created and connect with it. Then ask what is the life that I want?

What do my values need to be in order to create the ultimate vision for my life? What's most important to me in my life?

Very key questions like those will support you in discovering your values, so it is now time to choose them. Do not put this off! You can use the list provided or find other words. Again put pen to paper and write them down.

If you want to make money, discipline is required to make a difference and leave a legacy. Giving and contribution is needed.

## Choose 7-10 then pick your most important one!

Authenticity

Achievement

Adventure

Authority

Autonomy

Balance

Beauty

Boldness

Compassion

Challenge

Community

Competency

Contribution

Creativity

Curiosity

Determination

Fairness

Faith

Fame

Finances

Friendships

Fun

Growth

Happiness

Honesty

Humor

Influence

Inner Harmony

Justice

Kindness

Knowledge

Leadership

Learning

Love

Loyalty

Meaningful Work

Openness

Optimism

Peace

Power

Recognition

Religion

Reputation

Respect

Responsibility

Security

Self-Respect

Service

Spirituality

Stability

Success

Status

Trustworthiness

Wealth

Wisdom

**Create your Top Ten**

1. _____

2. _____

3. _____

4. _____

5. _____

6. _____

7. _____

8. _____

9. _____

10. _____

# GOLDEN GOALS

There are goals.. then there are GOLDEN goals! These are goals set up in a way that works where you are set up to WIN! The journey and process becomes a win too. Let's learn how, read below and let's go grow and glow!

Now one of the most important parts of staying fresh and staying blessed is stepping into an exciting, enticing future for yourself and believing you can achieve whatever it is. See I believe we can create whatever we want; we are indeed masters at turning the invisible visible. So here I will show you how to set goals and why.

**Most people don't succeed and achieve because they don't believe they can, and they rarely write their goals down or create a system to get there.** However the top 3% do, and that would be us.

Brian Tracy makes a great imagery of this. Imagine being given darts to throw, and your goal is hitting a bulls eye. The one without goals is at a disadvantage because he or she will be blindfolded, spun around in a circle five times and drunk! That's what it's like when you have no aim in life. The one with goals is sober, can see with fine vision and has been given an advanced course on dart throwing and has access to extra darts to throw. What an upper hand the one with goals got, huh?

Goals give you a target to aim at! So let's get clear, out of the haze and rise above our fog by getting closer to your purpose and focusing on what you want. Start to think about that now with no limits. What are your large BIG goals??? Start HUGE. Then reverse it! Go 10 years in the future—then 5, 3, 2, 1! It's fun, but starts to boil down the smaller goals to create that reality for yourself.

# 3 ACRONYMS TO SUPPORT YOU IN GOAL SETTING

WOOP from "Rethinking Positive thinking"
Wish Outcome Obstacle Plan
First
-Wish! What would you like to do? Start with just today.
-Outcome
What would you wish you could get done.. how would that feel!? Imagine completing it.
Let's not hesitate or procrastinate,,, which leads to potential challenges.
-Obstacle what could get in your way? Is it distractions or other obligations?
-Plan
If then
IF this "obstacle" comes up, THEN I will take this "action." Make an if-then statement, and you will be ready to achieve your goal with more ease.

Next GROWS
Goal Reality Opportunity Will and strengths
1st Redefine whatever the goal is
2nd Look at the truth in this moment. Face the reality of the gap in between. Then,
3rd Notice the opportunity of what's possible
4th Use your willpower to get started until you create a habit of action towards it
5th Leverage your strengths and the strengths of others to make it easier and more fun along the way!

Last but surely not least S.M.A.R.T.

Specific Measurable Attainable Realistic and Time bound goal!

I can't tell you how many people neglect this part of the process which is most important

Make sure your goal has the above qualities

Example

Let's say Bob is 160 pounds on February 20th. After his weak goal on New Years of losing eight didn't work, he creates a great goal here below:

"I am a fit trim warrior at 150 pounds by May 1st! And it was easy and fun!!"

Notice how it has all the elements of SMART with in it!

I'd like to also add that it was stated personally, positively and in the present tense. I request you really say it like it already happened. This pulls you toward the goal! It creates tension and puts you there as if it's done. Then next use the the other 2 tools above and review them daily and watch wonders happen with your action.

Here is space provided for you to play with what you want. Then use some of the process to synthesize your goals and create an action plan to fill the gap!

_____

_____

_____

_____

# Success Tracker

## Success Tracker

Connect back with the virtues you wrote about, which you will be living out. Will living in that way support you in attaining your goals. Are those goals true to you? It is always good to double check. If they are very opposite from your virtues and values, it will be very difficult to achieve them.

As humans we act in accordance with our identity. This is the fastest hack toward your goal you can ever give yourself!

Another strategy you can use to set yourself up to win is defining a successful day. By setting up the parameters and ground rules for what it takes for you to win each day, you'll feel super successful! To know you've had a great day by the time you're lying down in bed at night, what are the ways of being and actions you must engage in? For me it's simple:

**"I must live my values, accomplish the top 3 tasks, meditate at least 20 minutes, learn something, connect deeply with a minimum of 5 people and make a positive difference with 5 as well! Record the day in some way and have fun!"**
--Dougie Forlano

See! It's simpler than it seems! Now how about you !?

Write out what it takes. Make it doable day in and day out, so you can be a success daily and make it a stretch—or make it stretch?.

**My Successful Day:**

_____

_____

_____

_____

_____

_____

_____

_____

_____

_____

_____

# GRATITUDE

The power of gratitude is inescapable. It's the incredible invention and secret that god gifted us to tap into our limitlessness and truly experience bliss. No matter who you are or where you are using gratitude, this force will transform any negativity, resistance or fear in your life.

Einstein proved everything in the universe is energy. We too are energy, and, therefore, we vibrate at frequencies attuned to our thoughts, FEELINGS and behavior. This all ultimately stems from our Character, and that is what creates our destiny! Now what I will invite you to take on here is to see yourself as a Grateful person, and as you begin to identify with it, ask what do grateful individuals do? Well for one they GIVE, and they also are happy to receive because they get that there is grace in this word and blessings will come. My challenge for you here is to GIVE to yourself by writing down DAILY what you are thankful for. That's also something thankful people do, and I'm here today to tell you you are a gift; you are a grand gesture of greatness, and this tool of actively capturing blessings by writing them down on paper is a GAME CHANGER! I promise you. It not only works. It makes life easier, richer, and ultimately creates greater results!

The research is out on gratitude Journaling. Look it up! The bottom line is what you appreciate appreciates! Imagine if you want a new watch and were not thankful for the one you had that someone gave you. You'd then be sending out that dominant frequent frequency and rarely would attract something better. The same is true for your car, crib and RELATIONSHIPS.

So we can stay in the shit or shift out of the dissatisfaction, entitlement, jealousy, resentment and attachment. Therefore, add the F for focus and create the word shift instead, which enables one to shift into a life of light, ever-expanding love, by simplifying seeing the blessings and OF COURSE STAYING FRESH to the newness in our lives. With this awareness you can awaken aliveness and automatically start attracting more awesome results!

Seriously this isn't just some fairy dust I'm sprinkling on you: this is my experience. When I was in Pittsburgh on March 16th, 2015, I walked into a store called "Journeys of Life" and I bought a pocket sized green gratitude journal for just 8 bucks! And I wrote in it at least 3 times a day every day—usually even more often, and my life began to soar literally! I then interned for my dream mentor Elliott Hulse down in Florida. The next thing I knew is that with incredible practice I was flying off to live with multi-millionaires, maids & chefs for free in a $35 grand a month Hollywood Hills Mansion! And it got better! I met more dream mentors and started giving back and becoming a mentor to many others!

So yes it kind of works. Keeping a journal is the the brightest, most attractive and effective tool to achieve your goals! When you commit to writing what you're grateful for half a year, you will see the magic for yourself! Six months is about how long I journaled until I ended up in that magical mansion, from which I started proactively capturing and causing an environment of gratitude. In just under 3 months I was at Strength Camp in person with my online mentor. It has a lot to do with practicing thanksgiving and not just waiting around once a year for the holiday.

It all goes back to energy like I said in the beginning. It's physics. It's also social dynamics, showing others in the world. It's what works when you tap into giving the joyful truth of who you are. If you raise your frequency through this practice, you results around you will be in accordance.

Your vibe attracts your tribe, birds of a feather flock together, like attracts like, and it is law after all! People who are like themselves, so as an added bonus, your quality of relationships will boost too!

My mentor @Bigmike who was putting all that money into the mansion and now has only grown and expanded where he lives, what he is up to & the contribution he makes because he uses what's within this journal—@ Bigmike says that knowledge is not power, only APPLIED knowledge is power. So now you know it's up to you to DO.

What are you grateful for? I'll share some of what I have put on my list here:

I am thankful for having a working phone!
Fingers to type
Eyes to see
Clothes
A beating heart!
A car that can get me from point A to point B consistently
Every person I ever had the pleasure of connecting with
Every challenge I've ever had
Having traveled to over 40 states in the U.S.
The blue sky and clouds
The opportunity to share my thoughts, ideas and voice

It's your turn, and the more specific—the better!

_____

_____

_____

_____

_____

_____

_____

_____

## I am Grateful For:

_____

_____

_____

_____

_____

_____

_____

_____

_____

_____

_____

_____

_____

_____

_____

_____

_____

Here are some additional super fantastic strategies **to step up your gratitude habits.**

1.  Use the triple A method! Acknowledge, Accept and Appreciate
2.  Stop saying, I have to do something. Instead, say, I am BLESSED to! This one word is a game changer!
3.  Trade your expectations for appreciation!
4.  Use contrast. Think of the worst! Imagine how bad it can be or how tough others have or how you once had it and see your circumstances from that view
5.  Make, send and share thank you cards!
6.  Conduct a Gratitude RAMPAGE! Go off on a tangent for a minute of passion on everything you are thankful for! This one is fun!
7.  Tell someone a different person daily 3 things you are grateful for about them
8.  Below use the space to gratitude journal! It can be opportunities, experiences, environments, things, others and yourself! Jot it all down. The more you see and capture, the more you'll notice.

More space to collect the thanks to be given!

_____

_____

_____

_____

_____

_____

_____

_____

_____

_____

_____

_____

_____

## AFFIRMATIONS AND INCANTATIONS

100 years ago if we described what radios, laptops, cell phones are and how they work digitally connect to frequencies, you would think the person explaining it to you is nuts!!

I bet less than 100 years from now we will say the same thing about affirmations.

Incantation is another ball game. This is when you put emotion into it with your vocal tonality and body movements. It deepens the belief you are enforcing. Your mind will say "you're lying, that's not true." But when you do an incantation, your higher self talks back and says, "Bullshit! I am powerful!"

I am happy whole Perfect and complete
I am so blessed to have lovely relationships. The best is yet to come
My energy is off the charts
I am blessed to be my best
I am an incredible intelligence resourceful entrepreneur
I am a magnet attracting everything best for me and my family
I am super sensitive to serendipitous experiences
I have the perfect living space
What I want is still alive and achievable
I am worthy of whatever I wish simply because I am alive
I can feel love anytime I give it
I am happy whole Perfect and complete

I've got nothing to prove and nothing to hide so don't puff up or shrink down. Just be baby just breathe.

You now create your own and the key to making it an incantation is using your energy by moving your body and saying it with enthusiasm!!

## ACKNOWLEDGEMENT OF SELF

List all your wins and accomplishments small to BIG! This creates core confidence, better self esteem, a track record and proof you CAN do what you want. You also become less needing of validation from others. You will take more risks and play a larger game! Make your list of at least 50!

**My Wins and Accomplishments:**

_____

_____

_____

_____

_____

_____

_____

_____

_____

_____

## Success Tracker

_____

_____

_____

_____

_____

_____

_____

_____

_____

# FUTURE LETTER TO SELF AND TO ANOTHER

This exercise is designed to have you see your goals, lifestyle and dreams already accomplished! You are the person you want to be. You can do this now as if you are a month, half a year and a whole year into the future. You will write a thank you letter to yourself celebrating, encouraging and praising the current moment version of yourself. Use an entire page for this and don't hold back! I still look at mine in tough times!

The next letter you will write to someone in your life currently, thanking them for the difference they've made in your life! I recommend thank-you cards, but this is different. This is a thank you card to a family member, lover, friend or mentor a year out, saying thanks for who they are in your life and sharing with them what you have done! All your new exciting recent accomplishments. You don't need to give this to them. Feel free to text a picture of it to them so they can hold you accountable. The key to both of these letters is to not only visualize this future you, but imagine you are literally sitting down in gratitude writing this letter. Engage all your senses, put yourself there, and it's the same as actually sharing what you have done and become.

You can also do this on a daily basis to before you start each day. Write what you have already done as if it's night time and you're writing what happened. Go into detail around what you would like to occur this day. Then at the end of the day when you write what happened, you can see how close or off you were to what you predicted in your intention. You can see what was missing. Was it focus? Persistence? Belief that you could? Taking chance? Being responsible? And start seeing themes. Good luck and have fun! Make a great day and create a great life.

In the remainder of your book is your Journal! I invite you to write out what happens in your life. You can do it daily or weekly! I highly recommend the daily habit because this is how you truly get a pulse on your life and the system I and many other leaders have used. But don't beat yourself up if you miss a day. This requires discipline at first, but then it becomes a habit, and you become unstoppable!

Even a month is better than nothing. The point is to constantly check in with where you are in your life and to consistently level up, making sure your action are aligned with your purpose, values, goals and surroundings!

This is why it's recommended to take a highlighter and review you days, weeks and months, celebrating your wins acknowledging yourself and always learning from what is not working!

Before you blindly jump into writing what happens day to day, review all the insights you have created, reflected and recorded. Do this as often as you must. I recommend once a day and weekly will work too! Just writing it down gets you further than 90% of people who are aimlessly shooting for the stars. Last thing to do before you begin noting what happens each day is to project what you want every year from now by the month, week, and so on. Put spice in your life.

It's Your Year to steer
Making magic happen month to month
The Wonderful weeks ahead
Day to day dominance & delight
And Powers you put into the hours that make you say
WOWZERS!!

Again.

# DON'T NEGLECT TO REFLECT FROM YOUR DAILY JOURNALING

Sunday nights are great, but pick your time once a week to dedicate! Here's a few reasons why!

- It gives you perspective and attitude as if you're looking over your life at the top floor of a skyscraper!
- It boosts your confidence in discovery making
- It clarifies the big picture and
- It takes good experiences and deepens their lessons, turning painful experiences into successes by making them valuable opportunities to grow from

Also studies on habits prove that when you reflect after a certain activity, you will be automatically triggered to do something: it may be eating a yucky cookie, which fattens you OR putting to paper your thoughts about the day that you have just experienced.

Again this is for leaders ready to live their dreams, rock their world and take responsibility for themselves by nailing the details and finally finding a way to follow through on what they truly want. This gets you to go to the top, stay there, then, best of all, to have sooo much to give to others in return.

You can write however you like! Spell wrong, use slang, it does not matter as long as the habit is made and you are satisfied with it! I promise you if you do just half of what I'm asking here—YUP, that's right—just 50% of the practices suggested in this notebook of yours, the quality of your life will boost up like you would not believe, and so would your self-esteem. You'd be walking around awe-struck and in shock! I mean this in the best way possible: your life is about to get so great it will be weird. How awesome is this? But it's on you to create that by writing and filling your book up with your true expression.

# KEY SUGGESTIONS TO SOAK UP AND SINK IN THE SUCCESS TRACKER

Another suggestion is to add in your special success tracker a SUCCESS CHECKLIST for the day you will conquer tomorrow. Do this at the end of writing about each day.

You can also add in when you reflect

A Song/word/lesson of the week along with the top 3 things you did and 3 people you connected with!

A vital tool I put in the back of the journal is a space to collect and then share: QUOTES, JOKES AND/OR STORIES.

Another tool is A LIST OF Books to Read & Book reports on the major take-aways!

_____

_____

_____

_____

# DAILY JOURNALING

Remember, "The successful warrior is the average man, with laser-like focus."
— Bruce Lee

## Success check list

✓ _____

✓ _____

✓ _____

"To be great is to be misunderstood."
– Ralph Waldo Emerson

## Success check list

✓ _____

✓ _____

✓ _____

"Manage Activity and Focus on Results (MAFR)!"
– Adam Farfan

## Success check list

✓ _____

✓ _____

✓ _____

"Never stop being teachable. If you think you
know everything, you will never learn anything."
– Dani Johnson

## Success check list

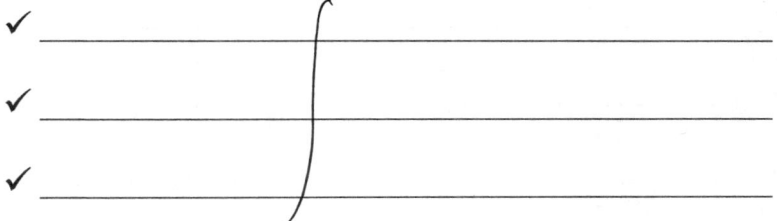

"Find yourself by losing yourself in the service of others." – Gandhi

## Success check list

✓ _____

✓ _____

✓ _____

"You have to be odd to be number one."
– Dr. Seuss

## Success check list

✓ _____

✓ _____

✓ _____

"To be great is to be misunderstood."
– Ralph Waldo Emerson

## Success check list

✓ _____

✓ _____

✓ _____

"Look within. Within is the fountain of good. It will bubble up if you dig." Dig in your mind and heart, and watch the greatness that emerges from it today. – Marcus Aurelius

## Success check list

✓ _____

✓ _____

✓ _____

"You can only learn from mistakes."
– Warren Buffett

## Success check list

✓ _____

✓ _____

✓ _____

"You must learn from mistakes of others. You can't possibly live long enough to make them all yourself." – Sam Levenson

## Success check list

✓ _____

✓ _____

✓ _____

"Faith keeps the person who keeps the faith."
Have faith that your life will unfold how you see fit.
See your success before you have it. Feed your
faith and starve your doubts. – Mother Theresa

## Success check list

✓ _____

✓ _____

✓ _____

"Promise me that you'll always remember, you
are braver than you believe, stronger than you
seem, and smarter than you think."
– Christopher Robin

## Success check list

✓ _____

✓ _____

✓ _____

"There is no illusion greater than fear." Smash
your fears into smithereens! – Lao Tzu

## Success check list

✓ _____

✓ _____

✓ _____

"Men are not afraid of things but how they view them." – Epictetus

## Success check list

✓ _____

✓ _____

✓ _____

"The only thing we have to fear is fear itself."
– Franklin D Roosevelt

# Success check list

✓ _____

✓ _____

✓ _____

"Always do what you are afraid to do."
– Ralph Waldo Emerson

## Success check list

✓ _____

✓ _____

✓ _____

"Don't wish it were easier, wish you were better."
– Jim Rohn

## Success check list

✓ _____

✓ _____

✓ _____

"Don't wish for less problems wish for more skills.
Don't wish for fewer challenges wish for more
wisdom." – Jim Rohn

## Success check list

✓ _____

✓ _____

✓ _____

"I learned that courage was not the absence of fear, but the TRIUMPH over it. The brave man is not he who does not feel afraid, but he who conquers that fear." – Nelson Mandela

## Success check list

✓ _____

✓ _____

✓ _____

"The book you don't read won't help."
– Jim Rohn

## Success check list

✓ _____

✓ _____

✓ _____

"The ladder of success is best climbed by stepping on the rungs of opportunity." – Ayn Rand

## Success check list

✓ _____

✓ _____

✓ _____

Remember, "some people want it to happen, some wish it would happen, others make it happen." – Michael Jordan

## Success check list

✓ _____

✓ _____

✓ _____

"I would maintain that thanks are the highest form of thought; and gratitude is happiness doubled by wonder." – G.K. Chesterton

## Success check list

✓ _____

✓ _____

✓ _____

"The more you learn, the more you earn."
Equally as important, Benjamin Franklin said, "An
investment in knowledge pays the best interest."
– Warren Buffett

## Success check list

✓ _____

✓ _____

✓ _____

"Give thanks for a little and you will find a lot."
– Hausa

## Success check list

✓ _____

✓ _____

✓ _____

"So sparkle and shine." The moment we let go of our fears and express ourselves, we empower others to do the same. – Barry Woods

## Success check list

✓ _____

✓ _____

✓ _____

"Failure is an event, not a person."
– Zig Ziglar

## Success check list

✓ _____

✓ _____

✓ _____

"Yesterday is history. Tomorrow is a mystery.
Today is a gift; that's why we call it the present."
– Bill Keane

## Success check list

✓ _____

✓ _____

✓ _____

"Become aware of just how rarely your attention is truly in the now. Knowing that you are not present is a great success. That knowing is presence." – Eckhart Tolle

## Success check list

✓ _____

✓ _____

✓ _____

"Set your goals high and don't stop until you get there." – Bo Jackson

## Success check list

✓ _____

✓ _____

✓ _____

"Nothing is impossible; there are ways that lead to everything, and if we had sufficient WILL we should always have sufficient means. It is often merely for an excuse that we say things are impossible."
– La Rochefoucauld

## Success check list

✓ _____

✓ _____

✓ _____

"Success is nothing more than a few disciplines repeated every day." – Jim Rohn

## Success check list

✓ _____

✓ _____

✓ _____

"Your attitude, not your aptitude, will determine your altitude." – Zig Ziglar

## Success check list

✓ _____

✓ _____

✓ _____

"If you count all your assets, you will always show a profit." – Robert Quillen

## Success check list

✓ _____

✓ _____

✓ _____

"Motivation is when you get a hold of an idea,
inspiration is when an idea gets a hold of you."
– Dr. Wayne Dyer

## Success check list

✓ _____

✓ _____

✓ _____

"Prepare when it's easy."
– Lao Tzu

## Success check list

✓ _____

✓ _____

✓ _____

"Will you look back on life and say, 'I wish I had,'
or 'I'm glad I did?'" – Zig Zigler

## Success check list

✓ _____

✓ _____

✓ _____

"What I regret most in my life are failures of kindness."
– George Saunders

## Success check list

✓ _____

✓ _____

✓ _____

"God will not have his work made manifest by cowards." How will you be bold, brave, and brazen today as you move forward?
– Ralph Waldo Emerson

## Success check list

✓ _____

✓ _____

✓ _____

"Early to bed, Early to rise, Makes you Healthy, Wealthy, and Wise." – Ben Franklin

## Success check list

✓ _____

✓ _____

✓ _____

"Behavior wags the tail of feelings."
— Moritist maxim

## Success check list

✓ _____

✓ _____

✓ _____

"Success depends upon previous preparation,
and without such preparation there is sure to be
failure." – Confucius

## Success check list

✓ _____

✓ _____

✓ _____

So many people prepare, get set and aim before they fire. In truth, you should fire then aim. Be prepared and remember, "You don't have to be great to start but you have to start to be great."
– Zig Ziglar

## Success check list

✓ _____

✓ _____

✓ _____

"Every skill you acquire doubles your odds for success." – Scott Adams

## Success check list

✓ _____

✓ _____

✓ _____

"Activity finishes the miracle process of turning nothing into something." – Jim Rohn

## Success check list

✓ _____

✓ _____

✓ _____

"God will not have his work made manifest by
cowards." – Ralph Waldo Emerson

## Success check list

✓ _____

✓ _____

✓ _____

"Have you ever gazed up into the infinity of space on a clear night, awestruck by the absolute stillness and inconceivable vastness of it? Have you listened, truly listened, to the sound of the mountain stream in the Forrest?" – Eckhart Tolle.

## Success check list

✓ _____

✓ _____

✓ _____

"Failure is good. It's fertilizer. Everything I've learned about coaching, I've learned from making mistakes." – Rick Pitino

## Success check list

✓ _____

✓ _____

✓ _____

"By three methods we may learn wisdom:
First, by reflection, which is noblest; Second,
by imitation, which is easiest; and third by
experience, which is the bitterest." – Confucius

## Success check list

✓ _____

✓ _____

✓ _____

"To skyrocket your success process, stop delaying, waiting, making excuses and looking to the future." – Greg O'Gallahger

## Success check list

✓ _____

✓ _____

✓ _____

Therefore, "Do not go where the path may lead, go instead where there is no path and leave a trail." – Ralph Waldo Emerson

## Success check list

✓ _____

✓ _____

✓ _____

"Discipline is the bridge between goals and
accomplishment." – Jim Rohn

## Success check list

✓ _____

✓ _____

✓ _____

"We can't change our destination overnight, but
you can change our direction."
– Jim Rohn

## Success check list

✓ _____

✓ _____

✓ _____

"We can't help everybody, but everybody can help someone." – Ronald Regan

## Success check list

✓ _____

✓ _____

✓ _____

"There is more treasure in books, than in all the
pirates' loot on Treasure Island."
– Walt Disney

## Success check list

✓ _____

✓ _____

✓ _____

"If you want resurrection, you must have crucifixion." – Joseph Campbell

## Success check list

✓ _____

✓ _____

✓ _____

"Do the thing you fear, and the death of fear is
certain." – Emerson

## Success check list

✓ _____

✓ _____

✓ _____

"Be who you are and say what you feel because those who mind don't matter and those who matter don't mind." – Dr. Seuss

## Success check list

✓ _____

✓ _____

✓ _____

"Always remember, that which gets measured–
gets managed." – Brandon Carter

## Success check list

✓ _____

✓ _____

✓ _____

"The person in the mirror is the toughest
opponent you are going to face."
– Rocky

## Success check list

✓ _____

✓ _____

✓ _____

"The mind is like a parachute: it only works if it's open." – Oscar Wilde

## Success check list

✓ _____

✓ _____

✓ _____

"One man with courage makes a majority."
– Andrew Jackson

## Success check list

✓ _____

✓ _____

✓ _____

"When we succeed, we party. When we fail, we
ponder." – Tony Robbins

## Success check list

✓ _____

✓ _____

✓ _____

"Losers are repeaters. Not only are they repeating their own mistakes, but they are also repeating the mistakes of their family and their culture. Winners have the courage to take what they learn. Make changes and make a difference."
– Julian Bradley

## Success check list

✓ _____

✓ _____

✓ _____

"We cannot change our past. We cannot change
the fact that people act in a certain way. We
cannot change the inevitable. The only thing we
can do is play on the one string we have, and
that is our attitude."
– Charles R. Swindoll

## Success check list

✓ _____

✓ _____

✓ _____

"You have to believe in yourself. You have to. You are your own product, so you have to believe in making you. There is a lot of head trash that we all carry around and you got to get rid of it." – Big Mike

## Success check list

✓ _____

✓ _____

✓ _____

"Success isn't magical or mysterious. It is the natural consequence of consistently applying the basic fundamentals." – Jim Rohn

## Success check list

✓ _____

✓ _____

✓ _____

"Affirmation without discipline is the beginning of delusion." – Jim Rohn

## Success check list

✓ _____

✓ _____

✓ _____

"You only get one life, but if you use it properly it is more than enough."– John C Maxwell

## Success check list

✓ _____

✓ _____

✓ _____

"I have slept and dreamt that life is joy. I awoke realizing that life is service. I acted on it and realized that service is joy." – Tagore

## Success check list

✓ _____

✓ _____

✓ _____

"An investment in knowledge always pays the
best interest." – Ben Franklin

## Success check list

✓ _____

✓ _____

✓ _____

"Before you check your likes on social media,
make sure you like yourself first."
– Lisa Nichols

## Success check list

✓ _____

✓ _____

✓ _____

"Your attitude, not your aptitude, will determine
your altitude." – Zig Ziglar

## Success check list

✓ _____

✓ _____

✓ _____

"Failure is not fatal, but failure to change might be." – John Wooden

## Success check list

✓ _____

✓ _____

✓ _____

"The world suffers a lot, and not because of
the violence of bad people, but because of the
silence of good people." – Napoleon Bonaparte

## Success check list

✓ _____

✓ _____

✓ _____

You may take a step back from time to time. However, don't dillydally around. "If you don't stand for something, you will fall for anything."
– Alexander Hamilton

## Success check list

✓ _____

✓ _____

✓ _____

"It's not what we do once in a while that shapes
our lives. It's what we do consistently."
– Tony Robbins

## Success check list

✓ _____

✓ _____

✓ _____

"The earth smiles and laughs in flowers."

– Ralph Waldo Emerson

## Success check list

✓ _____

✓ _____

✓ _____

"Even if you're on the right track you'll get run over if you sit there too long." – Will Rogers

## Success check list

✓ _____

✓ _____

✓ _____

"You are the average of the five people you spend the most time with." – Jim Rohn

## Success check list

✓ _____

✓ _____

✓ _____

"People who are unable to motivate themselves
must be content with mediocrity no matter how
impressive their talents are." – Andrew Carnegie

## Success check list

✓ _____

✓ _____

✓ _____

"Judge a man by his questions rather than his answers." – Voltaire

## Success check list

✓ _____

✓ _____

✓ _____

"You are a living magnet: what you attract into your life is in harmony with your dominant thoughts." – Brian Tracy

## Success check list

✓ _____

✓ _____

✓ _____

"The 'self-image' is the key to human personality
and human behavior. Change the self-image and
you change the personality and the behavior."
– Maxwell Maltz

## Success check list

✓ _____

✓ _____

✓ _____

"You can still do your best."
— Sean Combs

## Success check list

✓ _____

✓ _____

✓ _____

"Children astound me with their inquisitive minds.
The world is wide and mysterious to them, and
as they piece together the puzzle of life, they ask
'Why?' ceaselessly." – John C Maxwell

## Success check list

✓ _____

✓ _____

✓ _____

"The Future depends on what we do in the
present." – Gandhi

## Success check list

✓ _____

✓ _____

✓ _____

"I focus on my goals and try to ignore the rest."
– Venus Williams

## Success check list

✓ _____

✓ _____

✓ _____

"We constantly have to make a choice about how
we are going to feel. This is where it all begins."
– Elliott Hulse

## Success check list

✓ _____

✓ _____

✓ _____

"Successful people seek council and failures
listen to opinion." – John Schwartz

## Success check list

✓ _____

✓ _____

✓ _____

"People might not get all they work for, but they
must certainly work for all they get."
– Fredrick Douglas

## Success check list

✓ _____

✓ _____

✓ _____

"All the world's a stage; And all the men and women merely players; They have their exits and their entrances, And one man in his time plays many parts."– Shakespeare

## Success check list

✓ _____

✓ _____

✓ _____

"Under any circumstance, simply do your best
and you will avoid self-judgment, abuse and
regret." – Don Miguel Ruiz

## Success check list

✓ _____

✓ _____

✓ _____

"Leaders must invoke an alchemy of great vision"
– Henry Kissinger

## Success check list

✓ _____

✓ _____

✓ _____

"We cannot teach people anything. We can only
help them reveal it in themselves." – Galileo

## Success check list

✓ _____

✓ _____

✓ _____

"We all have two choices: We can make a living
or we can design a life. "– Jim Rohn

## Success check list

✓ _____

✓ _____

✓ _____

"Gratitude is a quality similar to electricity; it must be produced and discharged and used up in order to exist at all." – William Faulkner

## Success check list

✓ _____

✓ _____

✓ _____

"If you are not willing to risk the unusual, you will have to settle for the ordinary." – Jim Rohn

## Success check list

✓ _____

✓ _____

✓ _____

"Nothing great was ever achieved without enthusiasm." – Ralph Waldo Emerson

## Success check list

✓ _____

✓ _____

✓ _____

"Talent is a gift but character is a choice"
– John Maxwell

## Success check list

✓ _____

✓ _____

✓ _____

"Life takes on meaning when you become motivated, set goals and charge after them in an unstoppable manner." – Les Brown

## Success check list

✓ _____

✓ _____

✓ _____

# REMINDER
# KEY SUGGESTIONS TO SOAK UP AND SINK IN THE SUCCESS TRACKER

Other suggestions to add in your special success tracker is a Success Checklist for the day you will conquer tomorrow. Do this at the end of waiting about each day.

You can also add in when you reflect

A Song/word/lesson of the week along with the top 3 things you did and 3 people you connected with!

Some final vital tools I put in the back of the journal is a space to collect and then share

Quotes, jokes and or stories !

Then I have a list of

Books to read & short book reports on the major take aways!

## QUOTES TO COLLECT

_____

_____

_____

_____

_____

_____

_____

_____

_____

_____

_____

_____

_____

_____

## QUOTES TO COLLECT

## QUOTES TO COLLECT

_____

_____

_____

_____

_____

_____

_____

_____

_____

_____

_____

_____

_____

_____

# QUOTES TO COLLECT

# JOKES

# JOKES

## LYRICS/RAPS/POETRY

# LYRICS/RAPS/POETRY

# LYRICS/RAPS/POETRY

# LYRICS/RAPS/POETRY

# STORIES

# STORIES

_____

_____

_____

_____

_____

_____

_____

_____

_____

_____

_____

_____

_____

_____

_____

_____

# BOOKS I HAVE READ

# BOOKS TO READ

# BOOK REPORTS/BOOK NOTES

# BOOK REPORTS/BOOK NOTES

# BOOK REPORTS/BOOK NOTES

# BOOK REPORTS/BOOK NOTES

---

---

---

---

---

---

---

---

---

---

---

---

---

---

---

---

# BOOK REPORTS/BOOK NOTES

# BOOK REPORTS/BOOK NOTES

# BOOK REPORTS/BOOK NOTES

# BOOK REPORTS/BOOK NOTES

# BOOK REPORTS/BOOK NOTES

# BOOK REPORTS/BOOK NOTES

_____

_____

_____

_____

_____

_____

_____

_____

_____

_____

_____

_____

_____

_____

_____

_____

# BOOK REPORTS/BOOK NOTES

# BOOK REPORTS/BOOK NOTES

# ART WORK

# ART WORK

# ART WORK

## ART WORK

# MORNING AND NIGHT QUESTIONS

To empower you when your subconscious mind is most open and likely to be influenced

1. What am I grateful for? What else? Who can I thank today?
2. What am I excited for? How will I prepare today?
3. What am I committed to in my life right now?
4. Who do I love? Who loves me?
5. How can I live from my highest self today?
6. What can I do to even get a little bit better today?
7. What is the one thing I can do today such that by doing it, everything else will be made or unnecessary?
8. What will I give today?
9. How will I live today?

## NIGHT QUESTIONS BEFORE BED

1. What have I given today?
2. How can I do better?
3. What did I learn today?
4. What did I truly get from the day?
5. What can I acknowledge myself for today ?

6. Have I been thoughtful toward people today?

7. Would they express joy that they spent time with me?

8. How has today added to the quality of my life and others, and how can I use it as an investment in my future?

9. Did I live from my deepest values?

10. What was missing from today?

11. Did I do what I set out to do today? What distracted me? How can I stop it?

12. In my performance, what worked? What didn't?

# MORNING / NIGHT QUESTIONS

# MORNING / NIGHT QUESTIONS

# THE POWER OF FEEDBACK

What's the benefit in receiving honest direct FEEDBACK? First, feedback is just information that supports your results and effectiveness.

It turns out that getting an outside perspective on how you show up in the world is a game changer. With this awareness from others you can truly tap into your potential and adapt.

Do you really know how you come off to others?

You may say I don't care. However, go back to your vision: is hearing the truth worth it?

Receiving or from people that you know care enough not critics can cause rapid growth in any area of your life. Best of all it humbles you.

Also be a GIVER and tell others the truth on what works and what doesn't. Always ask for permission first and come from a loving place. This habit will have you be an even BIGGER leader and impact more lives.

Every single week constantly request feedback from those getting great results or people whom you know care enough about you to tell you the truth.

Then jot down what you hear here:

Acknowledge yourself for being humble enough to hear what is being experienced of you by others. It can be eye-opening for many. Yet when we identify our strengths and weaknesses, we can then build on them.

By the way, here is a the best formula I've come across for giving and receiving feedback.

What was good?
What can be better?
And what was the best?

Use those words, and you will become you own rockstar in the eyes of yourself and others.

# POWER OF FEEDBACK

# POWER OF FEEDBACK

# NUTRITION NOTES

Here is a space for you to either track what you eat or capture insights around the topic of what you put into your body. I put it here because it matters!

# NUTRITION NOTES

# NUTRITION NOTES

# NUTRITION NOTES

# NUTRITION NOTES

# DREAM JOTTING

This space is to record in detail anything and everything your remember about your dreams from sleeping the previous night. This is best done as soon as you awaken. This can give you greater understanding of your subconscious mind and awareness and answers to some of your challenges. It can also be very fascinating and interesting. I wouldn't always record my dreams, but when I do I am definitely glad I did.

I'm not going to go too deep into the benefits; however, I want to give you the space to capture your special dreams that may mean something. By the way, who creates this meaning? Yes, WE do. Therefore, why not plan for these enjoyable sweet dreams and whatever comes—to empower you. If they scare you, take it as a sign of more authentic action and give gratitude for your mind having your back.

# DREAM JOTTING

# DREAM JOTTING

_____

_____

_____

_____

_____

_____

_____

_____

_____

_____

_____

_____

_____

_____

_____

# DREAM JOTTING

# DREAM JOTTING

# DREAM JOTTING

# MEDITATIONS

Some form of Meditation is a MUST; the research is all out there !

This is a place for you to capture different methods which work for you and what opens up for you after you do your practice.

Many, including me, have discovered the best insights and ideas come to you when you create this space for yourself. Think about it before you go to sleep or in the shower. When you are away from your phone, have you ever noticed how more resourceful thoughts come to you? Well, it's time to take note of them to live an EPIC life!

# MEDITATIONS

# MEDITATIONS

_____

_____

_____

_____

_____

_____

_____

_____

_____

_____

_____

_____

_____

_____

_____

# MEDITATIONS

# IDEAS

It is an absolute must to block out a section and space for ideas. The ones that pop up in your head come out of hundreds of good ones—oftentimes more--thought about in a day. Some are extraordinary.

This will create more probability for clarity and action on them and identify which are the most important.

# IDEAS

# IDEAS

# IDEAS

## IDEAS

## IDEAS

## IDEAS

## IDEAS

# NOTES

# NOTES

## NOTES

## NOTES

## NOTES

# NOTES

## NOTES

# BOOK RECOMMENDATIONS:

1. *Awaken The Giant Within, Tony Robbins*
2. The Power of Now, Eckhart Tolle
3. The 4 Agreements, Don Miguel Ruiz
4. 7 Habits of Highly Successful People, Stephen Covey
5. Never Eat Alone, Keith Ferrazzi
6. The Way of the Peaceful Warrior, Dan Millman
7. New Earth, Eckhart Tolle
8. Steal Like an Artist, Austin Kleon
9. King Warrior Magician Lover
10. Levels of Energy, Frederick Dodson

When this journal is all filled up, take an action to celebrate on your commitment and continue this great habit of success and joy, so you can live your values, achieve you goals and purposes, and live in gratitude.

# ACKNOWLEDGMENTS

Editors:

Sal Marotta
Cedar Hansen
Nick Fuzzer
Alissa Coyle

Deep gratitude for mentors in my life such as:

Luke Faust
Michael Strasner
Leslie Stenger
Joe Martin
Steven Rowell
Elliott Hulse
Chris Barnard
Mark Dhamma
Mike Straumietis
Owen Cook
Eli Wilhide
Troy Casey
Larry Benet
Lewis Howes
Chris Bolger

Joe Henderson
Chris Hawker
Brandon Carter
Yahya Bakkar
Tai Lopez
Zedrick Clark
Damon Bingman
Briana Cribeyer

(Yes I have a ton of mentors. Nobody succeeds alone and my next book will be on mentorship!!)

Deepest thanks to my Family:

Father Joe Forlano
Big Brother Taylor Forlano
Mother Wendy Forlano
Sister Melody Forlano